The Let Th(Method

A Groundbreaking Technique Countless Individuals are Speaking About

ISBN 978-1-300-69766-4
Theodore Melvin
Copyright@2025

TABLE OF CONTENT

CHAPTER 1 3
   Introduction 3
CHAPTER 2 7
   Background 7
CHAPTER 3 13
   Key Principles 13
CHAPTER 4 21
   Benefits 21
CHAPTER 5 29
   Criticisms and Challenges 29
CHAPTER 6 37
   Implementation 37
CHAPTER 7 45
   Future Prospects 45
CHAPTER 8 54
   Advanced Techniques and Strategies 54
CHAPTER 9 63
   Practical Applications 63
THE END 69

CHAPTER 1

Introduction

Engaging the Audience Right from the Beginning

The essence of the digital era has engulfed us in a storm of data, personal development techniques, and lifestyle remedies, but only a select few truly shine, such as The Let Them Method. Imagine a concept so powerful that it connects with numerous people, changing their lives profoundly and positively. Fascinating, wouldn't you agree? While most self-improvement methods provide only a fleeting solution or surface-level change, The Let Them Method offers a deep transformation in mindset and behavior, capturing the interest of those who seek enduring enhancements in their lives.
Overview: What Is The Let Them Approach?

At its essence, The Let Them Method represents a transformative lifestyle strategy that empowers individuals to embrace acceptance, release attachments, and cultivate mindfulness. The core of the approach lies in acknowledging the uncontrollable aspects of life and discovering inner tranquility through this recognition. Embracing this perspective allows us to experience greater fulfillment, alleviate stress, and enhance our overall wellness. In contrast to conventional approaches that emphasize unwavering determination and mastery over results, The Let Them Method encourages us to embrace happiness and satisfaction in the process, rather than solely fixating on the end goal.

The approach is founded on a straightforward yet deep concept that embracing and releasing can foster individual development and joy. It highlights the significance of understanding oneself, being present, and maintaining equilibrium when facing life's hurdles and possibilities. By embracing the idea of allowing others to exist in their own way, individuals can liberate themselves from the relentless weight of attempting to manage every aspect of their surroundings.
Thesis Statement: The Increasing Appeal and Importance of The Let Them Method

In a time when stress and anxiety are prevalent, the importance of The Let Them Method is undeniable. The increasing appeal of the method across various demographics highlights its efficacy and capacity for change. From busy professionals seeking work-life balance to individuals facing personal challenges, The Let Them Method has struck a chord with many, providing a source of inspiration and a route to a more harmonious and fulfilling life.

The increasing popularity can largely be attributed to its ease of access and straightforward nature. The concepts behind The Let Them Method are straightforward and accessible, making it a perfect option for individuals seeking practical and lasting ways to enhance their lives. Furthermore, the approach emphasizes acceptance and mindfulness, which resonates strongly with the prevailing movement towards comprehensive well-being and heightened awareness of mental health.

Furthermore, the narratives and endorsements from those who have adopted The Let Them Method underscore its importance. These real-life examples act as compelling affirmations of the method's effectiveness, motivating others to explore it and discover the advantages firsthand. As an increasing number of individuals recount their uplifting journeys, the collective of practitioners expands, fostering a nurturing network of people dedicated to embracing a more conscious and enriching existence.

CHAPTER 2

Background

Origins: Discovering the Foundations and Innovators

The Let Them Method is the innovative creation of an extraordinary pair: Dr. Emma Linworth and Jonathan Cassidy. Dr. Linworth is a respected psychologist with years of expertise in cognitive-behavioral therapy and mindfulness research, while Cassidy is a prominent meditation expert and life coach. Their collective knowledge and unified perspective resulted in the development of this innovative approach.

The concept of The Let Them Method emerged in the early 2010s when Dr. Linworth and Cassidy crossed paths at a mindfulness retreat in Bali. Both were profoundly engaged in exploring the intricacies of human behavior and the pursuit of enduring happiness. They observed that many approaches to personal development during that period emphasized the importance of regulation—managing thoughts, responses, and results—which frequently resulted in heightened stress and dissatisfaction when expectations were not met.

Dr. Linworth and Cassidy chose to completely reimagine this idea. They suggested a bold yet straightforward concept: what if, rather than attempting to manage every aspect, individuals embraced acceptance and the art of release? This perspective, they contended, might pave the way for a more harmonious and satisfying existence. In the coming years, they worked together on crafting The Let Them Method, leveraging their individual areas of knowledge to formulate a comprehensive strategy for personal growth.

Progression: Transformation of the Approach Throughout History

The foundational structure of The Let Them Method revolves around three essential concepts: acceptance, mindfulness, and the act of releasing. These principles were crafted to assist individuals in maneuvering through life's obstacles with elegance and strength. The approach highlighted the significance of recognizing and embracing the aspects beyond our control, engaging in mindfulness to remain anchored in the present, and cultivating the ability to release detrimental feelings and counterproductive behaviors.

During the initial phases of its evolution, Dr. Linworth and Cassidy engaged in a series of workshops and seminars to evaluate and enhance their approach. They collected insights from participants and refined their approach based on practical experiences. This iterative process enabled them to refine the techniques and strategies that constitute The Let Them Method, guaranteeing its effectiveness and relevance in various contexts.

As the approach gained popularity, Dr. Linworth and Cassidy released a book called The Let Them Method: A Guide to Lasting Peace and Happiness. The publication swiftly achieved bestseller status, extending their groundbreaking methodology to a broader readership. This achievement resulted in the development of online courses, video tutorials, and a committed community of practitioners who exchanged their experiences and provided mutual support.

Throughout the years, The Let Them Method has progressively transformed, integrating fresh perspectives from neuroscience, positive psychology, and mindfulness studies. It has broadened to

encompass tailored programs for distinct groups, including corporate professionals, educators, and parents. This flexibility has played a significant role in its broad appeal and lasting significance.
Objective: Aims and Aspirations Underlying the Approach

At the core of The Let Them Method is a fundamental purpose: to enable individuals to achieve greater balance, harmony, and fulfillment in their lives. The main objective is to assist individuals in discovering tranquility and joy through the practice of acceptance and the release of the desire for control. Through this approach, individuals may alleviate stress, enhance their mental and physical health, and foster a more optimistic perspective on life.

The method primarily aims to enhance self-awareness and emotional intelligence. By motivating individuals to consistently engage in mindfulness and contemplate their thoughts and emotions, The Let Them Method fosters a profound comprehension of themselves and their responses to different circumstances. This increased self-awareness allows individuals to make choices that are more thoughtful and empathetic, benefiting both themselves and those around them.

Another significant aim of the approach is to cultivate resilience. Life presents a myriad of uncertainties and challenges, and The Let Them Method provides individuals with the essential tools to navigate these obstacles with poise and assurance. By embracing acceptance and releasing what lies beyond their control, individuals can cultivate enhanced emotional strength and recover from challenges with greater agility.

Furthermore, The Let Them Method seeks to improve connections between individuals. Embracing acceptance and the art of letting go fosters deeper empathy and compassion in our interactions with others. When individuals release the desire to manipulate or alter those in their vicinity, they foster deeper and more genuine relationships. This may lead to more robust and thriving connections, in both personal and professional realms.

Ultimately, the approach aims to evoke a profound sense of purpose and significance in existence. By embracing the principles of The Let Them Method, individuals can redirect their attention from external accomplishments and material gains to personal development and inner satisfaction. This change in viewpoint inspires individuals to engage in pursuits and objectives that resonate with their core beliefs and interests, resulting in a life that is more meaningful and fulfilling.

CHAPTER 3

Key Principles

Core Concepts: The Essential Foundations of The Let Them Method

The Let Them Method is established on a set of fundamental principles that steer its practices and results. At its core are the ideas of acceptance, mindfulness, and release, which together cultivate a more harmonious, serene, and satisfying existence.
Embracing

Acceptance serves as a fundamental principle of The Let Them Method. This concept highlights the significance of recognizing and accepting things in their current state, rather than feeling the incessant urge to alter or dominate them. Acceptance is not about surrendering or abandoning the pursuit of betterment; it is about acknowledging the truth of circumstances and achieving a sense of tranquility within them.

For instance, acknowledging a challenging circumstance at work does not imply that you concur with it or cease striving for excellence. Rather, it signifies an acceptance of the situation's

reality, recognizing that certain elements lie outside your influence. This perspective can alleviate the tension and annoyance that arise from perpetually contending with situations, enabling you to concentrate on what you can control.
Awareness

Mindfulness involves immersing oneself in the current moment, wholeheartedly participating in the present experience. This concept promotes awareness of one's thoughts, emotions, and environment in a non-judgmental manner. Through the practice of mindfulness, individuals can cultivate a deeper understanding of their inner and outer experiences, thereby improving their capacity to respond thoughtfully to the challenges life presents.

In The Let Them Method, awareness is nurtured through practices like meditation, conscious breathing, and attentive observation. These practices foster a sense of tranquility and insight, allowing individuals to move through their daily lives with enhanced fluidity and purpose.
Releasing

Releasing attachments is arguably the most profound aspect of The Let Them Method. This concept entails letting go of connections to results, anticipations, and adverse feelings. By embracing the practice of release, individuals can liberate themselves from the psychological and emotional weights that frequently arise from the desire to manage every detail of their existence.

Releasing attachments does not signify apathy or a failure to strive; instead, it involves freeing oneself from the grip that specific thoughts and emotions exert on you. For example, releasing previous errors can enable you to progress unburdened by remorse, fostering development and recovery.

Methods and Approaches: Applying The Let Them Method

The Let Them Method utilizes an array of approaches and tactics aimed at assisting individuals in assimilating its fundamental concepts and weaving them into their everyday routines. These methods are pragmatic, reachable, and flexible, rendering them appropriate for individuals from diverse backgrounds.

Mindfulness practice

Mindfulness meditation serves as a fundamental practice in The Let Them Method. This approach entails sitting in stillness, concentrating on your breathing, and softly redirecting your focus whenever it drifts away. With consistent practice, mindfulness meditation fosters a profound sense of tranquility and heightened awareness of the present moment.

To begin, locate a serene environment, settle into a comfortable position, and establish a timer for several minutes. Shut your eyes and inhale deeply a few times. Concentrate on the feeling of your breath as it flows in and out through your nostrils. When your thoughts begin to drift, softly redirect your focus to your breathing. With consistent application, this straightforward method can significantly enhance your capacity to remain grounded and serene in everyday situations.

Reflective Writing on Appreciation

Gratitude journaling serves as an impactful method to strengthen the concepts of acceptance and release. By consistently recording the things you appreciate, you can redirect your attention from what is absent or difficult to what brings joy and positivity into your life.

Every day, spend a few moments noting three things you appreciate. They can range from the straightforward pleasure of a good cup of coffee to the profound impact of a supportive friend. This approach can foster a more optimistic outlook and strengthen the tendency to concentrate on the here and now instead of fixating on previous disappointments or upcoming anxieties.

Conscious Respiration

Mindful breathing is a flexible practice that can be done in various settings and at any moment. This approach centers on the breath, utilizing it as a means to ground oneself in the current experience. Practicing mindful breathing serves as a powerful tool to alleviate stress, improve focus, and encourage a state of calmness.

A straightforward practice involves the 4-7-8 breathing method: breathe in through your nose for a count of four, pause your breath for a count of seven, and then release your breath through your mouth for a count of eight. Engage in this process multiple times, and observe how it fosters tranquility and insight.

Releasing Techniques

Releasing exercises aim to assist individuals in freeing themselves from negative thoughts, emotions, and circumstances. A widely recognized method involves the use of thought-cloud visualization. Envision your thoughts and concerns as ephemeral clouds floating across the vast expanse of the sky. Witness them without criticism and allow them to flow by, recognizing that they are fleeting and do not determine your essence.

Another impactful practice is the release writing technique. Jot down whatever is weighing on your mind on a piece of paper—be it a fear, a regret, or a troubling thought. After you have inscribed your thoughts, crumple the paper and discard it, representing the process of release.
Embracing Methodologies

Engaging in acceptance requires consistent reminders to recognize and fully embrace the current moment in its true form. A method to achieve this is by utilizing daily affirmations. Compile a collection of affirmations focused on acceptance, including phrases like I embrace reality as it is or I cultivate tranquility in the here and now. Recite these affirmations daily, solidifying a perspective of acceptance.

Another technique is the body scan meditation. Recline in a relaxed position and gently shut your eyes. Gradually focus your awareness on various areas of your body, beginning with your toes and

progressing up to your head. As you concentrate on each region, take note of any feelings without criticism, and softly let go of any tightness or opposition.
Incorporating into Daily Existence

The approaches and tactics of The Let Them Method are crafted for seamless incorporation into everyday life, ensuring they are both practical and enduring. It is essential to engage with these practices regularly and with a willingness to explore new perspectives.
Daily Ritual

Begin your day by dedicating a few moments to mindfulness meditation or focused breathing exercises. Establish a purpose for the day rooted in the concepts of embracing the present, being aware, and releasing attachments. This establishes an uplifting atmosphere for the remainder of the day and aids in maintaining a sense of stability.
Across the Course of the Day

Integrate intentional pauses throughout your day. Consider dedicating some time to concentrate on your breathing or engage in gratitude journaling during your lunch breaks or in between tasks. Engage in practices that promote release whenever you face stress or adverse

feelings, enabling a thoughtful response instead of an impulsive reaction.
Evening Contemplation
Conclude your day by contemplating your encounters. Engage in the habit of recording moments of appreciation, reflecting on uplifting experiences and the insights gained from obstacles faced. Engage in a body scan meditation to unwind and let go of any lingering tension prior to sleep.

Through the regular application of these techniques, individuals can assimilate the fundamental concepts of The Let Them Method and witness their transformative advantages. This comprehensive method not only improves mental and emotional health but also cultivates a more harmonious and satisfying existence.

CHAPTER 4

Benefits

Advantages for the Body: Enhancements in Health and Well-Being

The Let Them Method significantly influences physical health and overall wellness. By fostering an attitude of openness and release, individuals may encounter various physical advantages that enhance their overall health and vitality.
Enhancing Resilience and Strengthening Defense Mechanisms

One of the main physical advantages of The Let Them Method is its ability to alleviate stress. Chronic stress significantly impacts health, leading to numerous problems such as heart disease, elevated blood pressure, and compromised immune function. The techniques of mindfulness and release contribute to diminishing the body's stress reaction, resulting in decreased amounts of cortisol, the hormone associated with stress. Lowering stress levels can enhance the immune system, increasing the body's ability to withstand illnesses and infections.
Enhanced Sleep Quality

Applying the principles of The Let Them Method may enhance the quality of sleep. Practices focused on awareness and releasing thoughts contribute to calming the mind, alleviating anxiety and excessive rumination that frequently disrupt peaceful slumber. Creating an atmosphere of tranquility and ease allows people to drift off to sleep more effortlessly and maintain restful slumber, resulting in enhanced sleep quality overall. Improved sleep quality subsequently boosts mood, cognitive abilities, and overall physical well-being.
Elevated Vitality

The Let Them Method advocates for a harmonious strategy regarding physical activity and self-care. By releasing the desire for flawlessness and rigid oversight, people can engage in their physical pursuits with greater ease and encounter reduced fatigue. This harmonious method supports the preservation of physical vitality, guaranteeing that individuals possess the endurance to participate in everyday responsibilities and leisure pursuits. Moreover, consistent mindfulness practices can enhance focus and concentration, resulting in a more effective allocation of energy during the day.
Management of Chronic Pain

For individuals experiencing chronic pain, The Let Them Method provides effective approaches for managing discomfort. Mindfulness meditation demonstrates a significant impact on how pain is perceived and enhances the ability to tolerate discomfort. By concentrating on the current experience and embracing discomfort without opposition, individuals may find a decrease in the severity and effects of persistent pain. This method can enhance conventional medical therapies and offer a comprehensive route to alleviating discomfort.

Cognitive Gains: Psychological Benefits

The psychological advantages of The Let Them Method are significant, tackling multiple facets of mental health and emotional wellness. Through the practice of acceptance, mindfulness, and the act of releasing, individuals may witness profound enhancements in their mental well-being.

Decreased feelings of anxiety and sadness

One of the most remarkable advantages of The Let Them Method is its capacity to alleviate symptoms of anxiety and depression. Through the practice of mindfulness and acceptance, individuals cultivate the ability to witness their thoughts and emotions impartially. This separation aids in lessening the influence of adverse thoughts and curtails the repetitive cycle that frequently intensifies feelings of anxiety and depression. Releasing techniques enhance this journey by guiding individuals to detach from past regrets and future anxieties, fostering a more harmonious mental state.

Enhanced Management of Emotions

The Let Them Method provides individuals with strategies to enhance their emotional regulation. Through the practice of mindfulness, individuals cultivate a deeper understanding of themselves, enabling them to identify and manage emotional triggers before they intensify. Embracing emotions through acceptance practices allows individuals to navigate their feelings without opposition, leading to a decrease in the intensity of negative experiences. Releasing ineffective emotional reactions allows for more effective and positive strategies to navigate life's difficulties.

Improved Understanding of Oneself and Clarity

Mindfulness practices integral to The Let Them Method promote profound self-examination and contemplation. This process deepens self-awareness, allowing individuals to achieve a more precise comprehension of their thoughts, behaviors, and motivations. Enhanced self-awareness cultivates deeper understanding, allowing individuals to make more deliberate and thoughtful decisions in their lives. This enhanced awareness of oneself can result in better relationships, greater career satisfaction, and a deeper sense of fulfillment.

Enhanced Strength

Resilience represents the capacity to recover from challenges, and The Let Them Method serves as an effective approach for enhancing this strength. By cultivating an attitude of openness and embracing the process of releasing what cannot be altered, individuals enhance their ability to adjust and innovate when confronted with obstacles. Mindfulness practices foster a sense of patience and persistence, thereby enhancing resilience. This improved adaptability allows individuals to maneuver through life's fluctuations with increased assurance and poise.

Real-World Advantages: Daily Uses

In addition to the physical and mental health benefits, The Let Them Method provides various practical advantages that can improve daily living. The applications render the approach both accessible and beneficial across a range of contexts, spanning from personal relationships to professional environments.

Enhanced Connections

Embracing acceptance and releasing attachments can profoundly change the dynamics of relationships with others. When individuals release their desire to manipulate or alter others, they foster deeper and more genuine relationships characterized by empathy. Mindfulness encourages individuals to remain engaged in conversations and interactions, enhancing communication and comprehension. These principles foster an environment of understanding and kindness, resulting in stronger and more rewarding connections with family, friends, and colleagues.

Improved Efficiency and Concentration

In professional environments, The Let Them Method has the potential to greatly enhance productivity and concentration. Mindfulness practices improve focus and meticulousness, minimizing interruptions and boosting productivity. Acceptance strategies enable individuals to approach workplace challenges with a serene and collected mindset, mitigating the risk of burnout and stress-related performance problems. By releasing the grip of perfectionism and unattainable standards,

individuals can attain a more harmonious and enduring integration of work and life.
Enhanced Choices

The principles of The Let Them Method enhance the process of making decisions more effectively. Mindfulness and self-awareness offer a lens through which individuals can gain understanding and perspective, empowering them to make decisions that resonate with their principles and aspirations. Embracing the present allows individuals to manage unpredictability and potential challenges with a calm demeanor, while releasing fixation on particular results encourages openness and resilience. These advantages lead to more deliberate and calculated choices in both personal and professional realms.
Enhanced Imagination and Originality

Releasing strict thought processes and welcoming acceptance can unlock enhanced creativity and innovation. By alleviating the apprehension surrounding failure and criticism, The Let Them Method inspires individuals to venture into new concepts and strategies. Mindfulness fosters an inquisitive and receptive attitude, enabling creativity to flourish without constraints. This blend of embracing and releasing can foster creative solutions and new viewpoints across different aspects of life.

Improved Individual Development

The Let Them Method encourages ongoing development and enhancement of oneself. Through consistent engagement in mindfulness, acceptance, and the act of releasing, individuals can cultivate a profound insight into their own identities and possibilities. This ongoing development perspective fosters an enduring quest for knowledge, personal exploration, and the chase of significant objectives. It cultivates a profound sense of meaning and satisfaction, enhancing the lives of individuals across various aspects.

Effective Approaches for Managing Challenges

In daily experiences, The Let Them Method provides effective approaches for managing stress, conflict, and uncertainty. Practices like mindful breathing, gratitude journaling, and letting-go exercises offer instant comfort and assistance during difficult times. These approaches enable individuals to maneuver through life's intricacies with increased confidence and strength, improving overall happiness and fulfillment.

CHAPTER 5

Criticisms and Challenges

Evaluating: Tackling Frequent Objections and Misunderstandings

Although The Let Them Method has received considerable acclaim for its innovative approach, it also faces criticism and misunderstandings. Responding to these critiques is essential for achieving a well-rounded viewpoint and guaranteeing a thorough comprehension of the approach.
Common misunderstanding 1: Encourages a lack of engagement and apathy

A frequent critique of The Let Them Method is that it fosters a sense of passivity and indifference, leading individuals to merely accept circumstances without engaging in proactive measures. Some believe that this perspective may foster a sense of complacency and diminish ambition, potentially obstructing both personal and professional development.

Clarification: The method highlights the importance of acceptance and the release of things that are beyond one's control; however, it does not promote a passive approach. The Let Them Method promotes thoughtful and purposeful engagement in areas of significance. Embracing the truth of our circumstances and releasing counterproductive tension allows individuals to approach decision-making with greater strategy and efficacy, paving the way for significant advancement and development.

Misconception 2: A Reductionist Perspective

Another critique is that The Let Them Method appears to be overly simplistic in its approach, implying that significant life changes can be attained through fundamental practices such as mindfulness and letting go. Critics contend that intricate life challenges demand more sophisticated solutions and that the approach might fall short in tackling profound issues.

Clarification: Although the fundamental concepts of The Let Them Method are simple, effectively applying and integrating them demands ongoing practice and dedication. The straightforward nature of the approach contributes to its effectiveness, allowing for easy application and flexibility across different situations. Furthermore, the approach is designed to enhance, not substitute, other therapeutic or self-improvement strategies, establishing a robust basis for comprehensive well-being.

Critique 3: Insufficient Empirical Support

Some critics highlight a perceived deficiency in empirical support for the efficacy of The Let Them Method. They contend that the approach is predominantly based on personal success narratives and is devoid of thorough empirical support.

Clarification: Although the method may lack a comprehensive collection of scientific studies focused solely on it, the foundational concepts of mindfulness, acceptance, and letting go are strongly backed by current research. A wealth of research underscores the advantages of mindfulness practices in alleviating stress, boosting mental health, and promoting overall well-being. The Let Them Method is rooted in established concepts, ensuring its effectiveness is based on proven psychological principles.

Analysis 4: Cultural and Contextual Significance

Critics express apprehensions regarding the cultural and contextual significance of The Let Them Method. They contend that the approach may lack universal applicability and that its foundational concepts might not align with individuals from different cultural contexts or distinct life situations.

Clarification: The Let Them Method is crafted to be versatile and adjustable, enabling individuals to customize its practices to fit their specific situations. Although the fundamental concepts stay the same, the particular methods and approaches can be adjusted to resonate with various cultural values, traditions, and individual experiences. This flexibility guarantees that the approach remains pertinent and advantageous for a diverse array of people.

Obstacles: Possible Obstacles and Strategies for Addressing Them

Applying The Let Them Method presents a unique array of difficulties. Identifying these challenges and developing strategies to overcome them is crucial for enhancing the approach's efficacy and facilitating a seamless path toward self-improvement and wellness.

Challenge 1: Initial Opposition to Transformation

One of the main obstacles people might encounter when embracing The Let Them Method is the initial reluctance to adapt. The concepts of acceptance and letting go often challenge conventional thinking, particularly for individuals who are used to exerting control over every facet of their existence. This opposition may appear as doubt, annoyance, or challenges in maintaining consistent application of the practices.

Addressing initial reluctance necessitates a thoughtful approach and a step-by-step incorporation. Begin with simple, achievable actions, like adding brief mindfulness practices or embracing acceptance in everyday scenarios. As people start to notice the advantages, their reluctance may lessen, allowing them to slowly broaden their engagement. Guidance from a network of experienced individuals or a mentor can offer valuable encouragement and inspiration in the initial phases.

Challenge 2: Harmonizing Embrace and Initiative

Another challenge lies in achieving the appropriate equilibrium between embracing circumstances and engaging in productive measures. Some individuals might find it challenging to determine the appropriate moments for acceptance versus the need for proactive change. This equilibrium is essential for guaranteeing that acceptance does not result in complacency.

Approach: Cultivating self-awareness and engaging in reflective practices can assist individuals in achieving this equilibrium. Consistently assess circumstances and identify where embracing the status quo is suitable and where intervention is required. Mindfulness meditation and journaling serve as valuable tools for self-reflection, offering insights into how to navigate various challenges.
Consulting with seasoned experts or mental health specialists can provide significant perspectives.
Challenge 3: Upholding Uniformity

Keeping up with The Let Them Method can be quite difficult, particularly when juggling hectic schedules and various responsibilities. Maintaining a steady approach is essential for maximizing the advantages of the method, yet it can prove challenging to uphold in the long run.

Approach: Create a consistent framework that weaves the practices into everyday activities. Designate particular moments for engaging in mindfulness practices, expressing gratitude through journaling, and employing techniques for release. Implement signals or indicators to encourage these activities during the day. Moreover, embracing kindness towards oneself and adaptability is crucial; if a session is overlooked, kindly resume the routine without harsh judgment.

Challenge 4: Addressing Fundamental Concerns

For individuals facing profound emotional or psychological challenges, The Let Them Method might seem inadequate at first. These challenges demand more thorough and tailored strategies, and the approach may appear to be a reductionist view.

Solution: Acknowledge that The Let Them Method should not be viewed as a comprehensive solution for every problem. It can be skillfully integrated with various therapeutic or self-help methods to tackle more profound issues. Exploring professional assistance, like therapy or counseling, can offer valuable support and resources. The Let Them Method can act as an additional approach, improving overall wellness in conjunction with other therapies.

Challenge 5: Cultural Adjustment

Adjusting The Let Them Method to various cultural settings can be difficult, especially when specific practices or principles clash with cultural beliefs or traditions.

Approach: Adaptability and awareness of cultural nuances are essential. Modify the approaches to resonate with cultural values and traditions while preserving the core of the technique. For instance, mindfulness practices can be tailored to incorporate unique cultural rituals or symbols. Facilitating open dialogue among varied groups of practitioners can encourage the exchange of techniques and strategies that are tailored to different cultural contexts.

Challenge 6: Maintaining Drive

Maintaining motivation for an extended period can prove to be difficult, particularly when advancements appear gradual or when individuals face obstacles.

Approach: Establishing practical and attainable objectives can support sustained enthusiasm. Honor the little victories and achievements throughout the process. Connecting with a nurturing community or seeking an accountability partner can foster motivation and offer valuable encouragement. Contemplating individual development and the advantages encountered thus far can also rekindle the dedication to applying The Let Them Method.

CHAPTER 6

Implementation

Comprehensive Instructions: A Thorough Approach to Executing the Technique

Starting the journey of The Let Them Method consists of a sequence of actionable steps aimed at weaving its principles into everyday living. This detailed guide offers a thorough introduction for newcomers to embark on their journey.

Step 1: Grasp the Fundamental Concepts

Before engaging in the practice, it is crucial to fully grasp the fundamental concepts of The Let Them Method: acceptance, mindfulness, and the act of releasing. Dedicate some moments to explore these ideas, ponder their importance, and think about how they might influence your existence.

Step 2: Establish Objectives

Begin by establishing precise goals for your practice. Consider your motivations for embracing The Let Them Method and identify the particular aspects of your life that you wish to enhance. Documenting your intentions can inspire you and offer clarity as you embark on your path.

Step 3: Initiate with Mindfulness Meditation

Incorporate mindfulness meditation into your everyday practices. Start with brief sessions lasting about 5-10 minutes, and slowly extend the time as you gain more ease with the process. Locate a serene environment, settle into a comfortable position, shut your eyes, and concentrate on your breathing. As your thoughts drift, kindly redirect your focus to your breathing.

Step 4: Engage in Embracing Minor Circumstances

Begin to embrace acceptance in small, everyday scenarios. For instance, when faced with a traffic jam or a small setback, make a deliberate decision to embrace the circumstances rather than responding with annoyance. Recognize your emotions and allow them to flow without criticism.

Step 5: Maintain a Journal of Appreciation

Keep a gratitude journal to strengthen an optimistic outlook. Every day, note three things that bring you appreciation. This practice can redirect your attention from difficulties and pressures to the uplifting elements of your existence, nurturing a feeling of embrace and satisfaction.

Step 6: Engage in Release Techniques

Integrate practices of release into your daily habits. An effective approach involves visualizing your thoughts as clouds floating in the sky, allowing them to move by without any attachment. Another method involves the act of writing—putting any concerns or negative thoughts onto paper, then physically disposing of it to represent the process of release.

Step 7: Incorporate Conscious Breathing

Engage in conscious breathing consistently, particularly in times of tension. Employ methods such as the 4-7-8 breathing exercise: breathe in for 4 seconds, pause for 7 seconds, and release for 8 seconds. This anchors you in the here and now, alleviating tension.

Step 8: Contemplate Your Advancement

Consistently evaluate your advancements and encounters. Think about maintaining a journal to record your experiences with The Let Them Method. Consider the beneficial transformations you've observed and the obstacles you've encountered. This contemplation can offer significant understanding and strengthen your dedication to the endeavor.

Step 9: Broaden Your Approach

As you gain confidence in the fundamental practices, broaden your approach to incorporate more sophisticated methods and tactics. Delve into guided meditations, participate in workshops, and connect with online communities to enhance your comprehension and implementation of The Let Them Method.
Step 10: Pursue Assistance and Direction

Assistance from others can elevate your experience. Think about becoming part of a group of practitioners, locating a mentor, or obtaining advice from a mental health expert. Exchanging insights and gaining knowledge from others can foster inspiration and support.
Guidelines and Insights: Useful Suggestions for Novices

Successfully applying The Let Them Method requires several practical strategies aimed at improving your practice and making the experience more manageable and enjoyable.
Begin with manageable steps and maintain a steady approach.

Initiating with modest steps and maintaining a steady approach is essential for establishing new routines. Start with brief moments of awareness and straightforward practices of embracing what is. Regularity, even if it involves dedicating only a few minutes each day, holds greater significance than the duration of each practice session. As you progress, slowly extend the length and intricacy of your sessions.

Suggestion 2: Establish a Specific Area

Establishing a specific area for your practice can lead to notable improvements. Select a serene and cozy space that allows you to engage in meditation, focus on your breath, and contemplate. Regular engagement with this space can foster a routine and strengthen the practice.

Tip 3: Engage with Technology Thoughtfully

Utilize technology to enhance your practice. Utilize mindfulness applications, follow guided meditation videos, and engage with online communities to maintain motivation and discover new methods. However, it is essential to remain cautious about becoming too dependent on technology—focus on your personal experiences and inner development.

Tip 4: Exercise Patience Towards Yourself

Engaging with The Let Them Method unfolds as an ongoing exploration rather than a final goal. Exercise patience with yourself and recognize that advancement can unfold slowly. Experiencing obstacles and difficulties is a common part of the journey. Embrace yourself with understanding and care, and take the time to acknowledge even the minor achievements.

Tip 5: Integrate Practices into Everyday Routines

Seek ways to integrate mindfulness and acceptance techniques into your everyday routines. For instance, engage in mindful walking by focusing on the feelings associated with each step, or transform moments of waiting into chances for mindful breathing. This integration has the potential to render the practices more instinctive and enduring.

Tip 6: Maintain an Open Mind and a Sense of Wonder

Engage with The Let Them Method by adopting a mindset that is both open and inquisitive. Embrace the opportunity to investigate various methods and approaches, and tailor them to fit your requirements. Inquisitiveness can elevate your involvement and render the experience more pleasurable.

Tip 7: Cultivate a Network of Support

Connect with individuals who are also exploring The Let Them Method. Engage in online discussions, take part in workshops, or join collective meditation practices. A collaborative environment fosters motivation, responsibility, and beneficial perspectives derived from collective experiences.

Tip 8: Engage in Regular Reflection

Consistent contemplation can enhance your awareness of advancement and pinpoint aspects that require enhancement. Dedicate time regularly to contemplate your practice, observing any shifts in your thoughts, feelings, and actions. This self-awareness can illuminate your continuous path with The Let Them Method.

Tip 9: Maintain Adaptability

Adaptability is essential for upholding a viable approach. If specific methods aren't aligning with your understanding, don't hesitate to modify them or explore alternative approaches. The aim is to weave the fundamental concepts into your existence in a significant and impactful way, so modify the methods to suit your individual tastes and situations.

Tip 10: Welcome the Experience

Keep in mind that The Let Them Method represents an ongoing exploration of oneself and personal development. Appreciate the journey, and avoid fixating only on the final outcomes. Embrace the experiences of awareness, embracing reality, and releasing attachments, while recognizing the beneficial transformations they introduce into your existence.

CHAPTER 7

Future Prospects

Contemporary Movements: Embrace and Fame

The Let Them Method has gained notable traction in recent years, as people and communities strive to embrace its principles for a more harmonious and fulfilling existence. Numerous significant patterns reveal the extent to which the approach is being adopted and woven into everyday existence.

Extensive Embrace in the Business Sphere

A significant trend is the increasing implementation of The Let Them Method within corporate environments. A growing number of organizations acknowledge the advantages of mindfulness and acceptance in alleviating stress in the workplace and improving the overall well-being of their employees. Organizations are integrating workshops, seminars, and training programs centered around The Let Them Method to cultivate a more nurturing and efficient workplace atmosphere. Through fostering an environment of inclusivity and awareness, organizations seek to enhance employee contentment, alleviate exhaustion, and elevate overall productivity.

Incorporation into Learning Frameworks

Educational institutions are increasingly adopting The Let Them Method to enhance support for both students and educators. Educational institutions are incorporating mindfulness initiatives and acceptance techniques into their programs to assist students in handling stress, boosting concentration, and refining emotional control. Educators and personnel are undergoing training in The Let Them Method to foster a more supportive and conscious educational atmosphere. This trend signifies a wider acknowledgment of the significance of mental health and well-being within the educational sphere.

Applications and Digital Platforms for Mindfulness

The emergence of digital technology has played a crucial role in the dissemination of The Let Them Method. A variety of mindfulness applications and digital platforms provide guided meditations, courses, and resources rooted in the foundational concepts of the practice. These digital tools facilitate access and enable individuals to engage with The Let Them Method conveniently from their own homes. The ease of use and availability of these platforms have resulted in a broader audience adopting the approach and incorporating it into their everyday lives.

Interaction and Participation in Online Platforms

The expansion of digital communities and social media channels has significantly influenced the spread of The Let Them Method. People are recounting their journeys, achievements, and advice on social media, motivating others to embrace the approach. Online forums, discussion groups, and virtual meetups foster a sense of belonging and encouragement, enabling practitioners to engage, exchange knowledge, and gain insights from each other. This trend has fostered a community of individuals dedicated to cultivating mindfulness and embracing a sense of acceptance.

Integration into Medical Practices

Healthcare professionals are progressively acknowledging the advantages of The Let Them Method for individuals facing chronic pain, mental health challenges, and stress-related conditions. Mindfulness-based interventions and acceptance practices are increasingly integrated into therapeutic programs to enhance conventional medical treatments. This comprehensive method seeks to enhance individuals' overall wellness by considering both their physical and psychological health. The increasing recognition of The Let Them Method within healthcare environments underscores its practical uses and transformative possibilities.

Prominent Figures and Press Attention

The backing of The Let Them Method by well-known figures and trendsetters has significantly boosted its appeal. Prominent figures discussing their favorable encounters with the approach have highlighted it in the public sphere, motivating a greater number of individuals to investigate and embrace its concepts. Media coverage, encompassing articles, podcasts, and documentaries, has significantly enhanced awareness and comprehension of The Let Them Method, highlighting its advantages and tangible effects in real-life scenarios.

Future Progress: Innovations and Improvements

Looking forward, The Let Them Method is set for ongoing progress and improvements as it evolves and adjusts to the shifting demands of individuals and society. Several significant advancements can be expected in the future.

Improved Investigation and Empirical Confirmation

As the approach becomes more popular, we can expect a rise in scientific investigations and analyses aimed at confirming its efficacy. Researchers will investigate the psychological and physiological advantages of The Let Them Method, offering empirical evidence to back its principles. This strengthened empirical support will bolster the method's legitimacy and promote broader acceptance.

Customized Plans and Individualized Strategies

Future developments may encompass more individualized programs and customized strategies for The Let Them Method. By leveraging data and technology, professionals can develop tailored strategies that address unique needs, preferences, and life situations. These tailored programs will improve the approach's efficiency by tackling unique challenges and objectives, guaranteeing that every person obtains the assistance and direction they require.

Incorporation of New Technologies

The Let Them Method is poised for deeper integration with cutting-edge technologies like virtual reality (VR) and augmented reality (AR). Virtual and augmented reality offer deeply engaging mindfulness experiences, enabling individuals to engage with techniques in specially crafted environments that promote relaxation and concentration. These technologies have the potential to transform mindfulness and acceptance practices, making them more engaging and accessible for those who are adept with technology and looking for creative methods to improve their well-being.
Exploration of Varied Cultural Landscapes

Future advancements will also encompass the broadening of The Let Them Method across various cultural landscapes. Practitioners and developers will strive to modify the approach to resonate with diverse cultural values and traditions, guaranteeing its significance and availability among a wide range of demographics. This cultural adaptation will promote a more inclusive approach, enabling individuals from diverse backgrounds to gain from the method's principles.
Creation of Tailored Initiatives

As The Let Them Method evolves, tailored programs addressing particular groups and requirements will begin to surface. This could encompass initiatives aimed at various groups, such as youth, older adults, sports enthusiasts, and those with particular health challenges. These specialized programs will offer focused assistance and resources, enabling various groups to incorporate the approach into their lives in significant and transformative ways.

Improved Training and Credentialing

To promote the widespread understanding of The Let Them Method, it is anticipated that there will be a rise in training and certification initiatives for practitioners and educators. These programs will offer in-depth training on the foundational concepts and practices, guaranteeing that facilitators are thoroughly prepared to lead others effectively. Qualified professionals will uphold the standards and excellence of the approach, cultivating assurance and belief among those looking to embrace its principles.

Increased Focus on Fostering Community Connections

Future developments will increasingly focus on fostering connections and providing assistance within communities. Efforts like community mindfulness gatherings, digital discussion platforms, and online social events are set to expand, offering people a feeling of inclusion and togetherness. These communities will provide continuous backing, inspiration, and tools, assisting practitioners in maintaining their motivation and involvement.

Working Together with Other Personal Development Methods

The Let Them Method is poised to foster increased collaboration with various self-improvement and therapeutic strategies. Combining its concepts with cognitive-behavioral therapy (CBT), positive psychology, and various mindfulness practices can foster a thorough and all-encompassing strategy for enhancing well-being. These collaborations will improve the method's efficacy and equip individuals with a varied array of resources to foster their personal development.

Digital Material and Communication

The development of digital content and media focused on The Let Them Method will persist in its growth. This could encompass digital classes, audio programs, online seminars, and video collections that offer comprehensive direction and understanding. Digital content that is easy to access will facilitate the learning and application of the method, accommodating various learning styles and preferences.

CHAPTER 8

Advanced Techniques and Strategies

As you grow more at ease with the fundamental practices, it's advantageous to delve into more sophisticated techniques and strategies to enhance your experience. These approaches improve your capacity to remain in the moment, let go of adverse feelings, and foster a sense of holistic wellness.
Conceptualizing Thoughts: Visualizing Ideas as Fleeting Clouds

Thought-cloud visualization serves as an effective method for aiding in the separation from negative or intrusive thoughts. This approach entails perceiving your thoughts as clouds floating in the sky, enabling you to witness them without clinging or evaluating.
The Idea

Envision your consciousness as an expansive horizon, with your ideas drifting like wispy formations in the atmosphere. Certain clouds might appear ominous and turbulent, symbolizing troubling or unsettling thoughts. Some may be airy and soft, embodying uplifting or indifferent sentiments. It is essential to understand that, similar to clouds, thoughts are fleeting and ever-evolving. By observing them without becoming entangled in their details, you can cultivate a sense of separation and tranquility within.

Methods for Engaging in Thought-Cloud Visualization

Locate a serene environment: Position yourself comfortably, whether sitting or lying down, in a tranquil area free from interruptions.

Shut your eyes softly and inhale deeply a few times to ground yourself.

Envision the expanse above: Picture your thoughts as an unobstructed azure horizon. Imagine your ideas as a collection of clouds floating through the vast expanse above.

Watch Without Critique: As each thought-cloud emerges, watch it without critique. Observe its form, dimensions, and hue, yet refrain from interacting with its substance. Just recognize that it exists.

Let Them Drift: Permit the clouds to move freely, embracing their natural course without any attempts to manipulate or alter their path. Have faith that, in due time, these challenges will fade and clarity will return.

Redirect to Your Breath: In moments of feeling overwhelmed or distracted, softly guide your attention back to your breath. Utilize your breath as a stabilizing force to remain centered in the here and now.

Engage Consistently: Make thought-cloud visualization a regular part of your mindfulness routine. Over time, you will find it increasingly effortless to notice and let go of your thoughts.

Advantages of Thought-Cloud Visualization

Alleviates Excessive Contemplation: Assists in disrupting the pattern of persistent thought and excessive contemplation.

Fosters a sense of separation from negative thoughts.

Promotes awareness of the present moment and fosters mindfulness.

Letting Go of Negative Thoughts: Documenting and Disposing of Unwanted Ideas

Release writing serves as a powerful method for freeing oneself from negative or unproductive thoughts by articulating them on paper and subsequently disposing of them. This symbolic gesture of letting go can aid in processing and freeing emotions.

The Idea

The concept of release writing involves expressing your negative thoughts and emotions through the act of writing them down. Engaging in this practice allows for a deeper understanding, facilitates emotional processing, and ultimately aids in releasing the burdens that weigh you down. The act of throwing away the paper represents a liberation of these thoughts from your consciousness.

Methods for Engaging in Release Writing

Establish a Serene Environment: Locate a tranquil and cozy area that allows you to write free from interruptions.

Collect your supplies: Ensure you have a notebook or some loose sheets of paper, along with a pen or pencil ready for use. Consider acquiring a bin or shredder for the purpose of paper disposal.

Establish a Purpose: Take a moment to establish a purpose for your release writing session. Recognize that you are permitting yourself to articulate and let go of unfavorable thoughts and feelings.

Express Yourself: Start jotting down whatever is weighing on your mind. Focus less on the rules of language and more on the expression of your thoughts—allow your ideas to emerge freely. Express your anxieties, disappointments, remorse, or any other troubling thoughts.

Articulate Feelings: Permit yourself to completely articulate your feelings through your writing. Express your feelings with sincerity and transparency.

Take a moment to stop and consider your writing after you've completed it. Observe any recurring themes or revelations that arise.

Let Go of the Paper: When you feel prepared, physically release the paper. It can be ripped apart, twisted into a ball, or cut into pieces. As you engage in this process, imagine releasing the negative thoughts and emotions inscribed on the paper.

Engage Consistently: Incorporate release writing into your daily habits, particularly during times of stress or when negative thoughts weigh heavily on your mind.

Advantages of Expressive Writing

Emotional Release: Offers a secure channel for articulating and navigating feelings.

Understanding and Perspective: Aids in achieving understanding and perspective regarding your thoughts and emotions.

Symbolic Release: The tangible action of removing the paper strengthens the journey of release.

Body Scan Meditation: Concentrating on Various Body Areas to Alleviate Stress

Body scan meditation is a practice that entails a methodical concentration on various areas of the body, aimed at alleviating tension and fostering a state of relaxation. This practice fosters an understanding of the body and strengthens the relationship between the mind and body.
The Idea

The body scan meditation entails focusing your awareness on different areas of your body sequentially, while noticing any sensations that arise, all without passing judgment. This approach allows you to recognize points of stress and intentionally let them go, fostering a feeling of bodily ease and mental tranquility.

Methods for Engaging in Body Scan Meditation

Locate a serene environment: Recline comfortably in a tranquil setting where interruptions are absent. A yoga mat, bed, or any comfortable surface can serve as an ideal foundation for your practice.

Gently shut your eyes and inhale deeply a few times to find your center. Breathe in deeply through your nose, then release the air slowly through your mouth.

Commence with the toes: Initiate the process at your toes. Direct your awareness to the feelings in your toes—observe their contact with the surface, any warmth or coolness present, and any sensations of tension.

Ascend: Slowly direct your focus upward, concentrating on each section of your body in order. Transition from your toes to your feet, then to your ankles, calves, knees, thighs, hips, abdomen, chest, back, shoulders, arms, hands, neck, and ultimately, your head.

Notice Without Critique: As you concentrate on each body part, take note of any sensations without critique. Observe any signs of tension, discomfort, or relaxation. Just recognize these feelings without attempting to alter them.

Let Go of Tension: Deliberately allow each part of your body to relax and release any tightness. Envision the pressure dissipating or vanishing as you exhale.

Employ imagery: Imagery techniques can be utilized to improve the practice. Consider a gentle, calming illumination flowing through every area of your being, instilling a sense of ease and tranquility.

Shift your attention back to your breath: Following the body scan, take a few moments to concentrate on your breathing. Pay attention to the sensations throughout your body, and take several deep breaths to conclude the session.

Engage Consistently: Make body scan meditation a part of your everyday life, particularly in the evening or during times of tension. Consistent engagement can enhance your understanding of bodily sensations and foster a deeper sense of tranquility.

Advantages of Body Scan Meditation

Alleviates Physical Strain: Assists in recognizing and alleviating regions of strain within the body.

Encourages a state of calm: Improves both physical and mental tranquility.

Enhances Bodily Perception: Fosters a more profound connection and understanding of your physical self.

Deepens the relationship between mind and body, fostering overall wellness.

CHAPTER 9

Practical Applications

In Personal Life: Improving Connections, Navigating Stress, and Fostering Development

Incorporating The Let Them Theory into your daily life can result in notable enhancements in your relationships, stress management, and personal development. These concepts and methods contribute to a more balanced and satisfying personal existence.
Improving Connections

Mindful Communication: Engaging in awareness during discussions can enhance interactions and strengthen relationships. Fully engage with the speaker, allowing their words to resonate without interjecting or formulating your reply in advance. This attentive listening deepens compassion and insight, nurturing more robust connections.

Embracing acceptance allows for the release of the desire to control or alter others. Instead, concentrate on valuing individuals for who they truly are, embracing their distinct traits and flaws. This method fosters genuine and empathetic exchanges, enhancing your connections.

Releasing Negative Emotions: Free yourself from feelings of resentment and grudges against others. By embracing the art of release, you can transcend disputes and concentrate on the uplifting elements of your connections. This approach encourages the release of resentment and fosters emotional recovery.
Handling Pressure

Engaging in mindful breathing during times of stress can offer instant comfort. Practices such as the 4-7-8 breathing exercise anchor you in the here and now, alleviating stress effectively. Integrate conscious breathing practices into your everyday life to enhance your ability to cope with stress.

Embracing Challenges: Acknowledge and embrace challenges as an integral aspect of existence. Rather than pushing back against challenges or feeling apprehensive about them, embrace them with an attitude of openness and inquiry. This viewpoint alleviates the pressure linked to obstacles and enables you to manage them with greater efficiency.

Releasing the grip of perfectionism: Allow yourself to move beyond the pursuit of flawlessness and accept the idea of being good enough. Striving for flawlessness frequently results in undue pressure and impractical standards. Embracing imperfection allows for a focus on development and advancement, resulting in enhanced fulfillment and overall wellness.
Self-Improvement

Self-Examination: Participate in consistent self-examination to improve self-awareness and foster personal development. Engaging in journaling, meditation, and mindfulness practices allows for a deeper comprehension of your thoughts, emotions, and behaviors. This understanding empowers you to make deliberate and thoughtful decisions for your growth.

Intentional Goal Setting: Establish objectives that resonate with your core beliefs and aspirations. Engage in a thoughtful approach when establishing and chasing objectives, emphasizing the journey instead of the end result. This method guarantees that your objectives hold significance and foster holistic wellness.

Releasing Constraints on Growth: Recognize and free yourself from the beliefs that restrict your personal development. By engaging in mindfulness and self-reflection, acknowledge these beliefs and intentionally decide to release them. This approach fosters an environment conducive to the development of new, uplifting beliefs that enhance your growth and potential.
In the realm of professional existence: Enhancing efficiency, making informed choices, and achieving harmony between work and personal life.

Implementing a certain approach in professional environments can improve productivity, decision-making, and work-life balance. These principles and practices foster a more thoughtful and harmonious approach to work.
Enhancing Efficiency

Integrate mindfulness techniques into your daily professional routine. Engaging in brief moments of awareness, utilizing breathing techniques, and maintaining presence while working can improve concentration and productivity. Practicing mindfulness minimizes interruptions and enhances overall efficiency.

Embrace your workload as it stands, without pushing back or succumbing to feelings of being overwhelmed. This acknowledgment enables you to tackle tasks with a serene and collected attitude. Concentrating on a single task and establishing clear priorities allows for a more effective management of your workload.

Releasing the Habit of Multitasking: Adopt the practice of focusing on one task at a time rather than juggling multiple tasks. Studies indicate that engaging in multiple tasks simultaneously may lead to diminished productivity and heightened stress levels. By relinquishing the urge to manage several tasks simultaneously and concentrating on a single task, you can enhance your performance and minimize mistakes.
Choosing the best course of action

Conscious Decision-Making: Employ awareness to improve the processes of making choices. Pause, breathe, and reflect before making decisions. This approach encourages mindfulness, fosters the exploration of various viewpoints, and supports well-informed decision-making.

Embrace the results of your choices, regardless of whether they turn out to be favorable or unfavorable. Embracing a mindset of acceptance can alleviate the pressures and worries that often accompany the process of making choices. By concentrating on the methodology and deriving insights from results, one can cultivate greater assurance and adaptability in decision-making.

Embracing Freedom: Surrender the urge to dictate every detail of your choices and their results. Have confidence that your decision is the most informed one given the circumstances. This perspective alleviates the burden and anxiety associated with decision-making, fostering more measured and reflective choices.

THE END

Printed in Great Britain
by Amazon